P9-DNS-699

With each child, the world begins anew.

—The Midrash

PRAISE FOR WELCOMING WAYS

★ Reading of the loving ways each culture welcomes its littlest ones, truly makes me feel the embrace of the whole human race. I can hear the echoes of the ancients on every page of this delightful book. I think they are smiling.
—Shu Shu Costa, author of *Lotus Seeds and Lucky Stars: Asian Myths and Traditions about Pregnancy and Birthing* and *Wild Geese and Tea: An Asian-American Wedding Planner*

★ In *Welcoming Ways*, Andrea Gosline invites us to relearn the sacred ways of opening our hearts to the newborn. Drawing from various traditions, she offers a step-by-step manual to those in search of meaningful ways to reconnect with authentic values.
—Sobonfu Some´, author of *Welcoming Spirit Home*

★ A marvelous book of inspiring ceremonies to welcome the new baby with the love of the best world traditions. *Welcoming Ways* is a treasure—beautifully conceived and illustrated.
—Alexandra Stoddard, author of *Living a Beautiful Life* and *Mothers: a Celebration*

★ *Welcoming Ways* is a lovely and inspiring book which gives grace to the sanctity of new life across many cultures. A Tibetan father once told me how important it is to notice and mark each new development in a baby's life-the first smile, the first laugh, the first step. This book gives us ceremonies to celebrate the early special moments of a newborn's introduction to life, family, friends, and home.
—Edie Farwell, M.A., co-author of *The Tibetan Art of Parenting*

★ This book gives eloquent voice to every family's deep desire to welcome, comfort, and celebrate the children in their lives. In its ecumenical and multicultural approach, it is a profound and powerful gift for parents and children everywhere.
—Karin Evans, author of *The Lost Daughters of China*

★ One of my greatest memories of giving birth to my child was the blessing ceremony we were honored with. It is with joy that I recommend

this imaginative book of welcoming ceremonies. Andrea and Lisa offer us many new ways to celebrate the awesome transition to parenthood.
—Jennifer Louden, author of *The Woman's Comfort Book* and *The Woman's Retreat Book*

★ Welcoming a new soul into the arms of his or her family and friends is the perfect way to begin creating traditions that can be handed down through generations. This book is a beautiful introduction to the art and practice of celebrating life.
—Vimala McClure, author of *Infant Massage: A Handbook for Loving Parents*, *The Tao of Motherhood*, and *The Path of Parenting: 12 Principles to Guide Your Journey*.

★ There is no thing more worthy of "beginning well" than the life of a child. In *Welcoming Ways*, Andrea Gosline and Lisa Bossi have co-created beautiful ways to invoke the power of LOVE and PEACE into the lives of our children and our communities. Reading this book is nourishing to our souls and helps us return to living ritualized lives.
—Scout Cloud Lee, Ed.D, author of *The Circle is Sacred*

★ How wonderful to have a book full of cultural responses to the awesome passage into parenthood. For families to find their own unique heart beat is a special joy. To include the many differences in such a loving way is a tribute to all new babies and new families everywhere.
—Mimi Greisman, M.A. Ed., Early Childhood Educator, *Congregation Sherith Israel*

★ Honoring the arrival of our children through the celebrations in this must-read book can transform the way we think about our families, ourselves, and our connections to our communities.
   —Julie A. Keon, Certified Doula (DONA)

★ *Welcoming Ways* invites parents and their loved ones into a deeper, more conscious experience of "family." The intentions affirmed during these dynamic and loving ceremonies create a sense of welcome that will last a lifetime.
—Mary Knight, author of *Love Letters Before Birth and Beyond*

WELCOMING WAYS

Creating Your Baby's Welcome Ceremony

with the Wisdom of World Traditions

WRITTEN BY ANDREA ALBAN GOSLINE

ILLUSTRATED BY LISA BURNETT BOSSI

CEDCO PUBLISHING COMPANY

SAN RAFAEL, CALIFORNIA

ISBN 0-7683-2233-2

Text © 2000 Andrea Alban Gosline
Illustrations © 2000 Lisa Burnett Bossi
Design © 2000 Ambledance Studios
All rights reserved

AN AMBLEDANCE BOOK

Published in 2000 by Cedco Publishing Company
100 Pelican Way, San Rafael, California 94901
Library of Congress Cataloging - in - Publication Data available.
For a free Cedco Publishing catalog, please write to the address above,
or visit our website: www.cedco.com

Printed in Hong Kong

1 3 5 7 9 10 8 6 4 2

No part of this book may be reproduced in any manner whatsoever without
written permission except in the case of reprints in the context of reviews.

★ *Dedication* ★

Created with love for our children,

Jake, Lily, and Lila.

✦ ✦ ✦ ✦ *Table of Celebrations* ✦ ✦ ✦ ✦

A Welcoming World

And the child came gently
to the warm embrace of family.
And they kissed the child and sang
a welcome song, promising
to nurture, guide, and celebrate
this precious new life.
And their joyful song was heard
in every grateful home,
by sunlight and twilight,
in this moment and all moments:

We are glad you're alive.
You belong here with us.
Welcome home, tiny star.

*When we take
time to mark a passage,
we are dipping into the
river of life.*

—ROBIN HEERENS
LYSNE

Before my son was born, I daydreamed for countless hours about the magical moment of birth. I imagined the satisfying exertion of pushing, then releasing, my infant into the hands of my adoring husband. I anticipated the sensation of my baby cradled at my breast and Carl's lips kissing my forehead, as he whispered thanks for my courage in laboring to bring our child into the world.

I was certain I would want to tell my birth story to everyone who cared to listen and would describe in great detail how it felt the first time I looked upon Jacob, and years later, Lily, hoping for radiant health and ten fingers and toes. I believed I would find the words to express the totality of my feelings.

But there were *no* words. The awe, the mystery, the stirred emotions—the most profound I had yet experienced in my life—occurred in inexpressible moments.

As those first days passed, Carl and I searched for the perfect ceremony to mark the start of our son's life, to show how glad we were for the experience of sharing his journey's beginnings and his entrance into our family and community. We looked for a significant way to recognize and welcome him.

We consulted our Jewish prayer book but the words, though beautiful, seemed too religious and didn't speak to our hearts, which were brimming with wonder. We wanted our ceremony to be meaningful to our non-Jewish friends too. We hoped to weave in rituals from other cultures and time periods to underscore the sense of continuity that comes from repeating age-old actions and words.

Then Jacob's eighth day of life arrived, the day we were obligated by Jewish law to conduct his *bris*. Forty family members and dear friends watched as my father tenderly dripped blackberry wine onto Jacob's tongue while the *mohel* swiftly circumcised him.

Our Rabbi's words—the same ones spoken at every other bris—were sacred, and we were grateful for his wisdom, yet deep inside we were not satisfied. Jacob's godmother Amy read a poem by e.e. cummings, providing the only fresh touch to the evening.

We had wanted to personalize this momentous ceremony but had not found a guide to help us. Pulling words and rituals out of the air was not an option, especially then, when feeding, changing, sleeping, bonding—the tasks of new parenthood—were all this inexperienced and overwhelmed couple could handle so soon after birth.

Let us create anew the rituals of ancient significance, with respect for ideas that have borne the tests of time and openness to new ideas that reflect the needs of our own era.

— MARIANNE WILIAMSON

Eight years later and pregnant again, I was determined to imbue our second baby's welcome ceremony with the personality and perspective of our family. I planned a *simchat bat* (joy of the daughter) ceremony for Lily, well in advance of her birth. The words I wrote and the rituals I wove reflected the miracle of our new baby's senses. I honored Lily's closest relatives, especially her big brother Jacob and her godmother Lisa, with singing and reading roles. Our family and friends came together on a warm summer evening to witness, honor, and celebrate Lily's new life. Together we touched what was deepest in ourselves as we welcomed Lily into our circle of loved ones.

Four months later, Lisa and her husband Adrian welcomed their first child into the world. When Lila was two months old, they officially celebrated her new beginnings. On a sparkling January morning, they chose their favorite songs and readings from Irish, Sioux, and pagan traditions, as well as from Dr. Seuss' writings. With two beloved family members, they ventured to the beach where they had watched many magnificent sunsets during Lisa's pregnancy. Coincidentally when they arrived at the shore, a Tibetan purification ceremony had just started. They joined three monks and a circle of hundreds tossing the colored sand of a sacred mandala into the surf. Lisa returned a stone she had found on the day she went into labor back to the sea. Lila's small, private ceremony followed. The day was simple and spectacular.

These beautiful, sacred occasions were the seeds for *Welcoming Ways*, an inspirational resource for all new parents, siblings, and families. Included herein are welcome ceremonies that are joyous and profound and reflect the traditions of those who have walked before us.

*More important to me than
anything else, I wanted [my baby]
to feel welcomed to life on earth.
I wanted to receive him here
on this blue planet, with gentle
and open love to help ease this vast
transition for him.*

— MAREN TONDER HANSEN FROM
MOTHER-MYSTERIES

Your welcome ceremony may be as simple and private as whispered words from parent to baby, or as elaborate and communal as a naming ceremony with brunch for fifty. Regardless of the size of your guest list, I suggest you invite special neighbors too, since they will witness your child's daily life up close.

I believe the words we say, the promises we make, and the actions we take in our babies' first weeks will shape their lives — and ours — for all time. Our intentions now will bring a pivotal sense of meaning and direction to every future moment. In this spirit, I invite you to open fully to the promise of every new life and share this gift with a welcoming world.

Andrea Alban Gosline
San Francisco, CA ★ January 2000

Every baby deserves a loving welcome.

I have created nine timeless ceremonies, drawing from diverse traditions, that will bring special inspiration to your newborn's welcome celebration. Whether this baby is your first or your fourth, blood-related or adopted, invite your friends and family to actively participate as you rejoice in the miracle of your new child.

You may choose to use the ceremonies as they are or as templates, weaving together the parts of each that touch your heart. Feel free to personalize the words and rituals to fit your cultural style and add your own family's ethnic customs or religious traditions.

The answers to the following questions may elucidate themes that are most compelling to you as a parent, making it easier to select a ceremony.

★ What do I want my baby to see and hear first? ★ What do family and friendship mean to me? ★ What qualities do I possess that contribute to a happy family life? ★ How did my parents choose my name and what does my name mean? ★ What do I love most about life? ★ What is my greatest source of inspiration? ★ What would I do differently if I could begin again? ★ Who are the most important people in my life and why? ★ What is the legacy I received from my ancestors? ★ What wisdom do I wish to pass on to my children?

HONORS

Your ceremony will be most meaningful when you honor your loved ones with ceremonial duties. Below is a list of roles that you may wish to assign. I suggest that if children are present they should be invited to contribute their fresh outlook and youthful vibrancy.

★ Ringing a bell (to call the group to attention) ★ Carrying in the baby ★ Holding the baby ★ Welcoming the group and making introductions ★ Stating the intention or purpose of the occasion ★ Lighting the candles ★ Reciting the various blessings, toasts, invocations, pledges, and inspirations ★ Leading the rituals ★ Singing a song ★ Reading a poem ★ Organizing the refreshments ★ Leading the closing prayer

SACRED SPACE

Select a peaceful indoor or outdoor setting for your ceremony, such as your home or garden, the beach or other body of water, a park, the forest, a house of worship, or a mountain. Mark the area in some way to consecrate it as sacred space. You might light candles, cast a circle around the gathering with stones or seashells, play tranquil music, and decorate with flowers, photos, or artwork.

There was a time when many homes had altars dedicated to the house spirits or ancestors. Each chapter in *Welcoming Ways* includes a section on creating altars, based on the theme of the ceremony, along with suggestions of symbolic objects to be placed upon them.

DETAILS

Here is a streamlined approach to the inevitable details you will need to address.

★ THE DATE Choose a date and time for your ceremony that works with your family's new rhythm. Especially gauge the readiness of mother and baby to entertain a high-energy group of well-wishers. Although every culture and faith prescribes different times for presenting the baby, wait until the parents, siblings, and new baby are refreshed and have settled in.

★ INVITATIONS Utilize the same phone tree you used to announce the birth of your baby. "Invitation by grapevine" is an easy way to spread the word.

★ MUSIC Whether you choose timeless birth music like Brahm's *Lullaby*, sounds from the sea, Gregorian chants, a commissioned song, or a solitary soprano voice, your favorite musical pieces will enchant the celebration.

★ REFRESHMENTS Ask your guests to bring their favorite finger foods or a tray of sweets. Provide the basics: paper plates, utensils, napkins, beverages, and wine.

★ CREATING KEEPSAKES Consider creating a simple printed program outlining the order of the ceremony, song lyrics, inspirational or responsive reading text, and a list of the Honored Participants. If you have the time and creativity, add photos or graphics, or enlist the decorating skills of the children.

I suggest you make a videotape of the event in which each guest orates a message for the baby and new parents. You will view this precious keepsake time and again. Later, the video will be a touching and meaningful going-away gift when your child leaves home for the first time.

Name Tree

These are the names used in each chapter's ceremony text.

ONE: Jeffrey (JEFF-ree)

"divinely peaceful" (French)

TWO: Cara (KAH-ra)

"beloved" (Italian)

THREE: Alexander (al-ig-ZAN-der)

"protector of humanity" (Greek)

FOUR: Kioko (kee-oh-KOH)

"child who meets the world with happiness" (Japanese)

FIVE: Lucas (LOO-kiss)

"bringer of the light" (Latin)

SIX: Morgan (MORE-gin)

"by the sea" (Welsh)

SEVEN: Olivia (o-LIV-ee-a)

"peace and friendship" (Latin)

EIGHT: Elan (eh-LAHN)

"tree" (Hebrew)

NINE: Jun (joon)

"the truth of life; wisdom" (Chinese)

A Gentle Entrance

From the house where baby dances

From the mother's faithful heartbeat

From the gateway made of twilight

To the cradle made of dawn

In the light of home awaiting

In a hurry to be with you

We are waiting for this moment

We are waiting all around

And we cry when we receive you

And we kiss your tiny fingers

whispering

whispering

*Being present at
the birth of a child,
like witnessing
the clear morning after
an all-night rain,
makes the whole
miracle of creation
more real.*

— NANCY FUCHS

The story of my first baby's birth day springs to life in vivid detail each time I retell it. I remember searching his face in the moments after his arrival, amazed that I recognized him. We looked deeply at each other in the soft light and felt the heart strings tying us together forever. He listened intently to my soothing voice and heartbeat, nestled between my bare breasts. Later, he wrapped his tiny hand around his father's forefinger while the nurse bathed and swaddled him. Even the cacophony and conventions of the hospital did not muffle the bonding song of our new family.

Happy Birthday

This ceremony commemorates your baby's momentous first hours. The focus is on your intentions for his life and enhancing the bonding time. You may decide to conduct the ceremony immediately following delivery or wait a few days to recreate this gentle entrance—your baby's birthright.

Baby's Welcome

MOTHER *holds the newborn and says:*

We welcome you, Jeffrey [your baby's name], our cherished son. We are your parents and you are our greatest collaboration from this day forward. You have come from our hearts, into our arms. We have waited for you with love and longing. You are safe now. Welcome home, Jeffrey.

FATHER: You are now responsible for your breath as we are responsible for ours.

May you grow into a bright and lively child. May your life be full of meaning and good fortune. May you enjoy a long, prosperous life.

A TRANQUIL BIRTH SETTING

★ *Dim the lights.*

★ *Play a welcome song.*

★ *Guide the mother's hands to pull the baby out.*

★ *Place him on mother's chest.*

★ *Caress and bathe the baby.*

★ *Wrap him in soft cotton.*

★ *Hold him close.*

★ *Notice.*

★ *Whisper.*

We are here to be moved by the sounds of the world, the sacred reverberations rising and falling throughout the universe, inviting us to celebrate and sing, to dance with our raptures and ecstasies, to ponder sounds audible only in prayer. — MARY FORD-GRABOWSKY

First Words Prayer

PARENTS, *whisper your intentions for your baby's life in his right ear, then his left:*

We are your parents and we will care for you.

We promise to reveal the adventure of life.

We promise to love you unconditionally.

We promise to learn from your challenges and inspirations.

We promise to tell you the simple truth.

We promise to pay attention to each of your small moments.

We promise to slow to your wonderful pace.

We promise to embrace your hopes and dreams.

We promise to open our hearts fully to your love.

We promise to become a happy family

Singing the News Ritual

In Morocco, the women and children of the community announce the arrival of newborns by "singing the news." Invite your family to make music with their favorite instruments and noise makers. Or teach them a simple welcome song to enliven your gathering.

Day by Day
may we know thee
more clearly, love thee
more dearly and
follow thee more nearly,
day by day.

— RICHARD OF CHICHESTER
(1197-1253)

"Beautiful one,
beautiful one, welcome!"

— SUNG BY AFRICAN
WOMEN WHEN THEY HEAR
THE BABY'S FIRST CRY

Meditation for Touch

Focus on the sense of touch for the first twenty-four hours of your newborn's life. Suspend day-to-day activities and just "be" together. Cup your baby's head with your hand and linger there. Trace his eyebrows. Tap his nose. Kiss his lips. Whisper lullabies in his ear. Massage his chest and back. Count his fingers and toes, pulling gently. Envelop him in your arms. Touch every inch of your baby with love and admiration. Honor his brand-newness in your life.

How beautiful it is to do nothing, and then rest afterward.

—SPANISH PROVERB

Children's Good News Basket

Fill a basket with "goodies" that symbolize long life and good news such as lollipops, hard boiled eggs dyed red, chocolate baby shoes, chocolate cigars, and "It's a Boy" or "It's a Girl" souvenirs. Have the children pass these momentos out to your family, guests, and the birth team.

COMTEMPLATION

The sound most similar to a newborn's scream is the sound of children, which is why children in my village are required to cry out in confirmation of the newborn's arrival. This confirmation satisfies something in the psyche of the newborn, who is now ready to surrender to being present in this world.

—MALIDOMA PATRICE SOME' FROM *THE HEALING WISDOM OF AFRICA: FINDING LIFE PURPOSE THROUGH NATURE, RITUAL, AND COMMUNITY*

CRADLE BLESSING

As your baby falls asleep in his
new home, recite:

There are four corners to his bed,
Four angels at his head,
Bless the bed he lies upon,
Bless the evening, bless the dawn.
Moon and sun, bless me please,
And bless this house and family.

—ADAPTED FROM AN IRISH MIDWIVES'
BLESSING OF THE HOUSE

Once the children
were in the house
the air became more vivid
and more heated, every
object in the house grew
more alive.

— MARY GORDON

CREATING AN ALTAR

CRADLE ALTAR

Prepare your baby's cradle as a sacred,
welcoming space. Place in and
around it objects that hold special
meaning for your family.

★ Heirloom blanket
★ Child-safe, plastic mirror
to delight baby with his reflection
★ Wooden rattle ★ Musical stuffed
animal (just outside the crib)
★ Paper mobile ★ Windchimes
(outside the nursery window)
★ Faceted hanging crystal (inside the
nursery window)
★ Handmade children's art
(on the walls)

Inspirational Readings

Just as I watch a summer wind
rustle the leaves of the trees and
appreciate its beauty, or sit on the bank
of a river as it finds its way over and around
the rocks and branches, so I will watch you
...unfold before me, knowing that you have a
plan for life within you. I will watch and look
and listen in awe.

— TIAN DAYTON FROM *DAILY AFFIRMATIONS FOR PARENTS*

The ancient moment
you slip into welcoming hands,
joy spills from my eyes,
your fingers graze mother's cheek, me.
Tracing lines on your
barely etched palms,
I see your family waiting there.

"When Krishna's mother looked
inside his mouth, she saw in his
throat the night sky filled with
all the stars in the cosmos. She
saw "the far corners of the sky,
and the wind, and lightning, and
the orb of the Earth...and she
saw her own village and herself."

— ANNIE DILLARD FROM
FOR THE TIME BEING

W O R L D
C U S T O M S

★ When Navajo women are in the final stages of labor, an honored friend sings to the baby and beckons him out with an eagle-feather brush. The woman who received the baby gives the first bath, then molds his nose, head, and limbs to ensure healthy growth, a straight nose, and long limbs.

★ In Tibet, priority is given to the father's special place during the baby's birth. It is his sacred responsibility to be present with the mother and their other children to welcome their newborn into the world.

★ Filipinas leave a bamboo box open in the delivery room to catch the baby's first cry.

★ The Herero of southern Africa announce the arrival of a baby boy with a cry of, "Okauta" (little bow) and the arrival of a baby girl with "Okazeu" (the name of one of the bulbs which women gather for food).

★ In Borneo, the arrival of a baby is announced by beating a drum for all to hear.

★ Tibetan midwives put blessed butter on the tip of the baby's nose at birth to symbolize good health, longevity, and always having enough nourishing food to eat.

★ Wayapia of Guyana mothers wash their babies in streams of water that they have warmed in their mouths, and then blow the babies dry.

★ The Mossi of Burkina Faso sing hushed lullabies that list their newborns' entire family tree.

★ Yemeni mothers whisper these words to their new babies: "My little meat, my little fat, my little honey, my grasshopper, my tiny moon, light of my eyes."

★ In the Algerian-Moroccan Sahara Desert, midwives whisper a litany into the newborn's ear: "The master engendered the heavens, the day with its sun, the night with its stars, the moon, the rain, and the clouds."

Farewell Prayer

We rejoice and give thanks for the gift of new life we received today. May our sweet baby receive in his days, blessings of love, wisdom, health, and abundance. May he give back richly to each of us and bring us together soon in celebration.

A child's spirit is like a child,
you can never catch it by
running after it; you must stand still,
and, for love, it will soon
itself come back.

— ARTHUR MILLER

Protection Blessing

ELDER:
The earth is your mother,
she holds you.
The sky is your father,
he protects you.
We are together always.
We are always together.
There never was a time
when this was not so.
Blessed be.

— ADAPTED FROM
A NAVAJO LULLABY

Welcome Home

Walking in beauty,

may you come in sunshine.

Happily walking,

may you carry stars.

Seeing you coming,

the children are happy.

Seeing you coming,

the families rejoice.

May we always live here,

treasured and protected.

May we always love here,

honored and blessed.

Becoming Family

The house holds
childhood maternally
"in its arms."

— VANGIE BERGUM

As we carried our baby across the threshold and into the warm embrace of our house, we realized that these rooms would never be the same. Looking through eyes that had just witnessed splendor, we envisioned our baby sleeping, playing, eating, laughing, crying, prancing, and dreaming. The walls absorbed our hopes for her life, the floor boards absorbed our tears of awe, and this old house became a home. We settled in, exquisitely aware of every breath, every sound, every blessing. In those days of closeness and quiet, we thought about our roles as guides of a brand new family.

What are our dreams for our children? What do we hope to offer them? What will they teach us? This ceremony, honoring home and family, grew out of our contemplations.

A place will express itself through the human being just as it does through its wild flowers.

— LAWRENCE DURRELL

Family Welcome

CARA (KAH-ra) means "beloved." (LATIN)

Place an array of colored candles in a large candelabra with the same number of holders as guests in attendance. (A grouping of individual candleholders will work just as well.)

ONE PARENT *lights the first candle and says:*

We welcome our family and friends and thank you for being here today to celebrate the birth of Cara [your baby's name]. We thank Cara for bringing us together in joy. We ask each of you to  watch over our family, keep us strong, and help us protect, love, and guide Cara through her life.

PARENT *invites the next guest to light a candle from the first one and says:*

The lighting of our family candelabra symbolizes the unity, diversity, and strength of our family life.

Each subsequent guest lights his or her candle from the one that was lit just before.

TRUE HOME RITUAL

Silently lead your guests through your home. Circle a sage stick or incense above your head and let the scented smoke waft into the four corners of each room. (Many cultures purify their living spaces this way.) Go back into the family room and say this blessing:

Today we open our hearts to Cara and give her a true home. Let us love each other boundlessly and build a strong foundation for our family within these protective walls.

Family Wisdom Ritual

ELDER: Many different life perspectives are represented at this gathering. Each of us has been a member of a family at one time or another. Let us offer to Cara, her siblings [names], and her parents, [names] the family wisdom we have collected throughout our lives.

Ask your guests to step up to the candelabra and share a thought about what family means to them and the wisdom they've gleaned from being part of a close community.

Inspirational Reading

RETURNING TO LIFE

This birth, this new life is not our first meeting, nor is this our first home. The welcome our hearts sing to you, oh round-faced one, has echoed down a thousand years. Here we are again, old friend, falling in love with you. Teach us your ways so that we may create ourselves anew. Teach us how to wonder and to play, to greet the day with eyes so wide open that the world falls in. Teach us how to let go of everything that isn't love, oh infinite, beautiful soul of our soul, one more time, so that we may know who we are.

— MARY KNIGHT, AUTHOR OF *LOVE LETTERS BEFORE BIRTH AND BEYOND*

It is right that families should be contented in the home, that there should be children living there, vigourous and healthy as young olive trees.

— ADAPTED FROM
PSALM 128

28

New Family Pledge

The youngest children in the group pass out flowers to the guests and everyone gathers around the family altar.

PARENTS *face each other, join hands and say:*

I promise to hear you, help you, and honor you with my greatest support and attention. I promise to care for you lovingly, so together we can take care of this family we both cherish.

PARENTS *turn to the new baby [and older children] and say:*

We promise to hear you, help you, and honor you with our greatest support and attention. We promise to care for you lovingly, so we can take care of this family we cherish together.

One by one, guests place their flowers in the vase, stating their intentions for how they will support this new family.

WELCOME

In Twenty-one Languages

Arabic: *marhaban*

Bulgarian: *dobre doshyl*

Chinese *(mandarin): shou huaying de*

Czech: *vitejte*

Danish: *velkommen*

Filipino: *bati*

French: *bienvenu*

German: *willkommen*

Greek: *kalosorisate*

Hebrew: *shalom*

Hungarian: *istenhozta*

Italian: *benvenuto*

Japanese: *yokoso*

Korean: *hwan yong*

Polish: *witamy*

Portuguese: *boas vindas*

Russian: *npuem (nuh-pi-awm)*

Sign Language *(American): The hand brings something in towards the body to show that someone is being invited to come forth.*

Spanish: *bienvenida(o)*

Thai: *kor*

Turkish: *karsilama*

BLESSING

God bless all those that I love;
all those that love me;
all those that love those
that I love;
and all those that love those
that love me.

— FROM AN EMBROIDERED
NEW ENGLAND SAMPLER
(16TH OR 17TH CENTURY)

When there is room
in the heart, there is
room in the house.

— DANISH PROVERB

CREATING
AN ALTAR

FAMILY ALTAR

Designate a space in your family's favorite gathering
spot for this "ode" to family. Drape a small table,
wall shelf, or mantel with a cloth the color of the
season. Arrange objects on the altar that symbolize
what family means to you:

★ Mirror (truth and wisdom)
★ Candelabra (illumination)
★ Pair of shoes (our path through life)
★ Candid family photos
(togetherness and spontaneity)
★ Tree branch from your backyard (strength)
★ Bird's nest (nurturance)
★ Vase (home)

Invocation to Parenthood

MOTHER *lifts a glass filled with wine or juice and says:*

I am a parent now. I will create my family with devotion, commitment, and great love.

I toast [name of partner] and thank you for helping me bring forth new life.

I toast Cara and [names of new baby's siblings] and thank you for making us a family.

Children's Wish Gallery

Provide paper and drawing implements for the children of the family. Suggest that they draw pictures of the games they hope to play with the new baby. Ask them to write a wish for the baby's house on the picture. Put up the "wish gallery" in the nursery.

❧ SIMPLE GESTURE ❧

At your first meal together as a family, light a candle for your baby from a pair of parent candles.

COMTEMPLATION

A child receives a history and culture from his family, and his identity, values, world view, and life habits are profoundly influenced by his experience of growing up in a particular family. Elders see in their families the way that their individual lives will extend forward in time. In the life of the family, past and future meet.

— THOMAS MOORE, FROM
CARE OF THE SOUL

WORLD
CUSTOMS

★ As soon as an Ainu (Northern Japanese) child is born, the father or grandfather whittles a stick of willow into a fetish, as he sits by the hearth—the heart of his home. When the fetish is ready, he sets it next to the baby's cradle as the tutelary god of his new child.

★ Ancient Romans hung olive branches from their front doors to announce newborn boys, and pieces of woolen fabric to announce girls.

★ In Korea, it is customary to erect a rice stalk in front of the house. If the baby is a boy, a dried red pepper is placed on the stalk. If the baby is a girl, a piece of wooden charcoal is used.

★ In Ugandan villages, the entire community gathers together singing and dancing when a baby is born. The father goes from house to house and receives congratulations. The mother and new baby wait at the entrance of their home to receive villagers as they stop by to express their good wishes.

★ When a baby is born in parts of Asia, the ritual called winnowing is performed to bond her to the family and home. The baby is placed on a tray, along with items representing characteristics, skills, and hopes for her future. A respected family friend raises the child up while catching the tray as it falls. Pieces of sacred thread are tied around the infant's wrists and ankles, to welcome her into the world as a traditional blessing is recited.

★ The first time an infant girl is laid in her cradle is celebrated in several Central Asian Jewish communities. In Bokhara, for example, small children participate in snatching away the sweet treats that have been placed around the baby in the cradle.

★ Koma of Cameroon grandfathers make tiny bows and shoot tiny arrows towards their newborn grandchildren while reciting a prayer of thanks to welcome them.

★ Around the world, round foods such as pears, grapes, pomegranates, bread, and moon cakes are eaten at baby welcome celebrations to symbolize family unity.

Closing Blessing

The time for leaving draws near.
We hold hands and remember
the gifts of today —
a new life, a new family,
a new circle of friends.
We give thanks for these gifts
and we hope that tomorrow
will bring us back together again.

My little one!
My sweet one!
My little girl!
You're only a baby,
But the time
To play with you, my baby,
Will go by quickly,
My little one!
My charming little bit of woman!

—SIOUX LULLABY

*We create our own
traditions for the same
reason we create our own
families. To know
where we belong.*

—ELLEN GOODMAN

Honor the Name

my name whispers

eternity

like rain

falling

down in the wind

bathing lightly

the leaves

falling

down on the breath of love

dwelling within me

behind me, before me

my name

in the trees

below

in the sky

above

Write your blessed

name upon my heart,

there to remain so

indelibly engraved that

no prosperity, no adversity

shall ever move me

from your love.

— THOMAS A KEMPIS,
GERMAN MONK
(1380-1471)

My name, Andrea means "feminine grace" and was given to me at my birth in 1959 by my parents. They carefully and thoughtfully chose my name to honor my father's mother. By the time I took possession of it, my name already

Mark of Recognition

had a life of its own, layered with strength and tenderness. It has since become just as much a part of me as my eyes and my hands. When I say my name aloud, I sing the song of my identity. When others address me by name, I am recognized. Because of my name, I carry my family with me wherever I go.

This naming ceremony celebrates the gift of a "good name" and the honor and identity we bestow upon our babies when we make public their heritage and parentage.

I have called you by name, now you belong to me.

— ISAIAH 43:1

Naming Ceremony

[sample]

MOTHER: Today we welcome our son into our family and honor him with the gift of his name, Alexander [your baby's name]. He is named in loving remembrance of my grandfather, Andrew [namesake and short description of his impact on your life] whom I never had a chance to meet but feel as though I know well from the stories told to me as a young girl. My grandfather was a journalist in Shanghai, China and admired as a kind, gentle, and strong man. He loved to watch the everchanging sea from a lounge chair at the beach. My hope is that Alexander will inherit from my grandfather the qualities of kindness, strength, curiosity, and the ability to communicate articulately.

ALEXANDER (AL-IG-ZAN-DER) means "protector of humanity." (GREEK)

FATHER: I welcome our son, Alexander into our family and give him the gift of our family names: Gosline and Alban. [Describe the roots of the parents' family names.] The Goslines are descendants of French Hugenots named Gosselin. When they immigrated to Pennsylvania from France, they anglicized their last name. The Alban name was chosen out of a phone book by

continued on page 39

FLOWER
SYMBOLS

Crocus: *Cheerfulness*

Dahlia: *Dignity*

Gladiolus: *Strength of*
Character

Hawthorn: *Hope*

Orchid: *Beauty*

Periwinkle: *Friendship*

Rose: *Love*

Sweet Pea: *Lasting Pleasure*

Violet: *Faithfulness*

Water Lily: *Eloquence*

White Chrysanthemum:
Truth

White Rose: *Simplicity*

Yellow Jasmine: *Grace*

—FROM *THE LANGUAGE OF*
FLOWERS BY GAIL HARVEY

CREATING
AN ALTAR

Cover a small table, wall shelf, or mantel with
a hand-me-down baby blanket, preferably one
belonging to your baby's namesake.

Adorn the altar with:

★ flowers that symbolize the hope
you hold for your baby's life

★ a candle inscribed with the baby's name
spelled out in seed pearls

★ framed parchment calligraphed with the
baby's name and its meaning

★ potted evergreen plant for his nursery

★ packet of wildflower seeds
to be scattered in the spring
in an open space

Andrea's father, after he graduated from medical school, to replace his difficult-to-pronounce Ukranian name, Abramovitch.

MOTHER: We have chosen Alexander's mentors, [names] who have promised to be a strong presence in our son's life and have vowed to acknowledge and celebrate this child.

MENTOR(S): With great honor, we accept the responsibility of guiding Alexander as he carries on the legacy of his namesakes and lives a fulfilling life, distinguished by his proud heritage.

ELDER: Bless these parents, Andrea and Carl [parents' names] and their newborn son, Alexander. May they treasure each other and may they together enjoy life as a family.

PARENT: Let us hold hands and give thanks silently for the loved ones we remembered today. [Moment of silence.] May our names become guideposts for the lives of our children. Bless Alexander with these sweet gifts.

...What we are doing is affirming that it is good to live, and that the gift of life is a good gift. We are saying our pleasure in the sun that warms our body, the wind that invigorates us, the rain that refreshes us. We are saying our rapture in...the ennoblements of love, the catharsis of creating, the joys of simple gestures of our everyday living. And as we do, we take into our arms that which is loved, and by "articulate breath," imprint a name upon the waiting future.

—CARL SEABURG, FROM *GREAT OCCASIONS: READINGS FOR THE CELEBRATION OF BIRTH, COMING-OF-AGE, MARRIAGE, AND DEATH*

W O R L D

C U S T O M S

★ Eskimo: A female elder calls out appropriate names while the mother is in labor, assuming that when the baby hears "it's" name, it will readily emerge from the womb.

★ Siberia: The baby is believed to be born without its name soul. During the baby's baptism, the name soul hears the call, rushes to the newborn's house to enter the baby's body and join the life soul, the sleep soul, and the linking soul.

★ Africa (West): Elders and babies are valued equally since they share a proximity with the ancestor's world—from which the newborn has just arrived and the elder is preparing to go. Sometimes an elder will call a baby "Grandpa" or "Grandma" to show deep respect.

★ Ghana: In addition to a name, a baby is given a song by his mother, inspired by the characteristics of his birthplace and the day of the week on which he was born.

★ Roman Catholic: Babies are often named after saints who are believed to bring strength to the child from God.

★ Sikh: A name is chosen for the baby that begins with the first letter of a random reading from the Guru Granth Sahib (holy book containing guidance and inspiration).

★ Tibet: Babies are given secret names by a *lama* (high priest) which are written down on paper, placed in a pouch and worn around the neck for life.

★ Bali: Each baby's name is considered a very personal piece of property. Balinese rarely say their names aloud; some elderly Balinese are the only ones who know their own names.

★ Muslim: On the seventh day of life, a baby's *Aqiqah* (name-giving) ceremony is performed, for which his body is carefully washed and his head is shaved.

★ Senegal: Prayers from the Koran are written on pieces of paper, then soaked in water. Small pieces of the paper are torn off and placed on the infant's tongue. On the seventh day of life, the baby's name is whispered three times into each of his ears.

Family Line Invocation

Chart your baby's ancestry as far back through the family line as you can, noting the name of each maternal and paternal predecessor, the number of children they parented, their occupation, and their favorite pastime.

PARENTS *alternate reading the lines of this invocation:*

[sample] You are Alexander, the Alban and Gosline families' newest, beloved member.

⋆ Alexander, you are the son of Andrea Elisabeth Alban, mother of two, poet and nature-watcher. ⋆ You are the son of Carl Edwin Gosline III, father of two, graphic designer and lover of the sea. ⋆ You are the grandson of Donna Lorraine Alban, mother of two, homemaker and choir member. ⋆ You are the grandson of the late Lucille Crawford Gosline, mother of three, teacher and rock collector. ⋆ You are the grandson of Jan Alban, father of two, pediatrician and stamp collector. ⋆ You are the grandson of the late Carl Edwin Gosline, Jr, father of three, teacher, coach, and craftsman.

Some of us look on as others name their children who in turn name their own lives, devising their own flags from their parents' cloth.

— RICHARD P. BRICKER

Gift of the Name Ritual

Ask your guests in advance to look up the meaning of their names. When they arrive, have them enter this information in your baby book or a special keepsake "name" journal. Ring a bell to call for silence and pass the book around the gathering. Each person reads his or her name, explains its meaning, and gives the name as a gift to the baby.

[samples]

* My name, Cam, is an English Gypsy name meaning "one who is deeply loved." I hope Alexander will receive an abundance of love and give it back happily to the world.

* My name is Sachi, which means "blessing," or "lucky" in Japanese. May Alexander enjoy every blessing he receives and lead a lucky life.

* My name Patrick is derived from Latin and means "royal character." According to legend, Saint Patrick cleared Ireland of snakes. I hope Alexander will possess noble qualities and be strong enough to overcome the challenges he faces.

* I am Irene. My name means "bestowing peace" in Greek. I give the gift of peace to Alexander and hope that he will work to make the world more peaceful.

Children's Friendship Circle

Arrange the children in a circle around the baby and his parents. Provide drums, noisemakers, and rattles. Begin the rhythm softly in unison. Allow the beat to grow faster and stronger then lighten again. The rhythm is symbolic of the heartbeat that connects us with each other.

CHILDREN *call out their names one by one, then say in unison:*

We welcome you, Alexander. We are your first friends.

Closing Blessing

HONORED FRIEND:
We thank our parents, providers of fair love,
knowledge, and undying hope.
They bring eternity to us—their children— and
we are named in their honor.
We walk together while they are upon this earth
and fill ourselves with their wisdom,
for their legacy is sweeter than the honeycomb.

—ADAPTED FROM THE APOCRYPHA

Awakening the Senses

I look into her eyes and remember

how the moon illuminates mountains.

I taste her tears and remember

where the ocean refreshes the shore.

I listen to her song and remember

what the wind sings in the evening.

I smell her hair and remember

why flowers bloom at dawn.

I touch her skin and rejoice

as the sun awakens the world.

...When you touch life,
touch it deeply so that
we may feel through your
fingertips the memories of
the beautiful earth.

— ONAUBINISAY
WAUBEZHAYSHEE

Celebrating Wonder

Watch a child playing in the park. At first, she is pure motion, scouting for treasure in the landscape of her day. And then, an amazing discovery catches her eye, and she grows still, holding her breath, watching a caterpillar inch by or a cloud shaping itself magically. She hears a bird call and stops to listen for the reply. She counts ripples on the pond and once again bursts into activity, rushing to catch the insect skating away on the smooth surface. She comes home humming, bringing her rich experience in hands covered with dirt, having truly tasted the day's delights. She reminds us of miracles—how our ability to see, hear, smell, touch, and taste enhances every moment we live.

This ceremony focuses our appreciation on our baby's five senses. As we learn to see the world's wonders through the eyes of our children, we look and listen more deeply and celebrate the pleasure of this awakening.

Candle Lighting

Ask your guests in advance to bring a colored candle from home. Ring a bell to announce the start of the ceremony. Guests stand in a circle around the parents and baby. Mother lights a pair of pink candles on the ceremonial table.

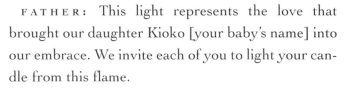

CANDLE
COLOR SYMBOLS

* Blue: *Peace*
* Green: *Hope*
* Orange: *Comraderie*
* Pink: *Love*
* Purple: *Comfort*
* Red: *Courage*
* White: *Purity*

FATHER: This light represents the love that brought our daughter Kioko [your baby's name] into our embrace. We invite each of you to light your candle from this flame.

MOTHER: May the brightness of our celebration circle follow Kioko wherever she goes.

Welcome Address

PARENT: We welcome you, family and friends, to the celebration of Kioko's birth. Your presence now helps us rejoice and honor her. We hope that after you leave today, you will continue to be a part of Kioko's life—to watch her grow and blossom.

GRANDPARENT: Kioko, we have waited for you and now we welcome you. We fill you with our love and we give you our time. Together we will listen to the singing birds, breathe in the fragrant air, and watch the world silently in awe.

Everything has its
wonders, even darkness
and silence, and
I learn, whatever state
I may be in,
therein to be content.

— HELEN KELLER

I face the distant peaks
of Chin, Country blue
and still after rain, Trees
merging into far twilight,
Smells of grass blown into
my cave, Who would want
a life beyond this?
Here, around us, endless
beauty. Now, around us,
endless wonder.

— INSCRIBED ON A TEMPLE,
HAN HUNG
(CHINA, EIGHTH CENTURY)

CREATING
AN ALTAR

Drape a small table, wall shelf, or mantel
with a textured cloth and place on it the following
objects, symbolic of our five senses:

★ white candle (sight) ★ goblet filled with sweet
wine (taste) ★ music box (sound)
★ sprig of aromatic flowers (smell)
★ crystal bowl filled with scented water (touch)

Place the altar in the middle of your ceremonial space
for use in the following ceremony.

I pray for the young mother
who is bringing new life to the people —
bless her and her baby
with health and serenity.
I pray for the small child,
new to the earth walk —
bless this new life with all things good.

— CHEYENNE BLESSING

Awakening the Five Senses Ceremony

MOTHER: I awaken Kioko's sense of sight with the light of this candle. (Light white candle.) Women have kindled the spiritual flame for home and family since ancient times. May Kioko experience the warmth and caring of community and share her enlightenment with everyone she meets.

FATHER: I awaken Kioko's sense of taste with this drop of sweet wine. (Place a drop of wine on baby's tongue.) Nature provides the fruit we transform into wine. We thank the earth for this gift. May Kioko be nourished by the abundance nature gives us and take pleasure in her gifts.

GRANDPARENT: I awaken Kioko's sense of sound with this welcome song. (Sing a favorite short melody or wind up the music box.) Music encircles us with a symphony of celebration. May the sound of blessing caress Kioko's

Children, like animals, use all their senses to discover the world.

— EUDORA WELTY

ears and fill her heart.

AUNT OR UNCLE: I awaken Kioko's sense of smell with these flowers. (Pass aromatic flowers beneath baby's nose.) The sense of smell brings our awareness to the essence of life and reminds us of the soul. May the flowers' fragrance surround Kioko and cultivate her spirit.

SIBLINGS: We awaken Kioko's sense of touch with this water. (Wash baby's hands.) Water bathes us in truth and hope. May Kioko immerse herself in the sea of life and enjoy this new beginning.

WORLD CUSTOMS

★ Tibetan Buddhists put objects on shrines in their homes and temples to symbolize the senses: shells (sound), food (taste), flowers (sight), incense (smell), and water (touch).

★ *Hana Matsuri* is the Japanese flower festival which celebrates the birth of Buddha, who was supposedly born in a grove of flowers. To show reverence for his life and teachings, followers place images of the young Buddha in floral shrines.

★ An elder of the the Blood Indian tribe (North America) paints the sign of the tribe on the baby's face with red ocher (earth). Then the baby is held up to the sun with the hope that light will follow the child through life.

★ Chinese celebrants, incorporate noise (gongs, cymbals and drums) and light (firecrackers) into their revelry.

BIRTHDAY OF THE GODS

★ *Rama Naumi* is a Hindu festival that celebrates the birthday of the god Rama, hero of the *Ramayana*. The Ramayana is an epic story that models ideal Hindu life. An image of baby Rama is set up in the temple and his worshippers bring offerings to the cradle.

★ Buddhists mark the birthday of Buddha by ceremonially washing images of him as an infant in sweet tea.

★ The birth of Krishna is similarly celebrated. His image is washed with yogurt, ghee (clarified butter), honey, and milk, then placed on a swing for all to take turns pushing. The sweet yogurt mixture is collected and shared with the guests.

Children's Promise

Invite the children to make a circle around the altar.

OLDEST CHILD:

I will do my best to be kind to Kioko. ★ I will do my best to be patient with her. ★ I will do my best to help Kioko grow up. ★ I will do my best to share with her what I love about life. ★ I will do my best to help Kioko be happy and feel welcome here.

Encourage the rest of the children to add their own promises.

Children's Nature Walk

Take a walk outdoors. Bring magnify-ing glasses and baskets. Gather shells, stones, flowers, driftwood, leaves, feath-

ers, acorns, and such. Carry your treasures home to the baby. Together glue the nature elements to a wreath for the front door. Or make a sculpture out of clay embedded with the most colorful, tex-tured objects. Each child takes one found object home to remember the intentions and gifts bestowed on this special welcoming day.

Closing Reading

We [are thankful] for this earth, our home; for the wide sky and the blessed sun, for the salt sea and the running water, for the everlasting hills and the never-resting winds, for trees and the com-mon grass underfoot. We [are thankful] for our senses by which we hear the songs of the birds, and see the splendour of the summer fields, and taste of the autumn fruits, and rejoice in the feel of the snow, and the smell of the breath of spring.

— WALTER RAUSCHENBUSCH
(1861-1918)

Abundant Blessings

Table ripe and brimming

With roses, loaves, and wine

Candles dance for lullabies

Hear their dozy hum

Moments sweet and savored

Words for wishing well

Blessings for a baby's grace

In gratitude we dwell

The family meal...is a custom that can enrich our knowledge of our historic roots by carefully prepared food from our own ethnic tradition, that can enlarge our love of literature by readings of poetry easily adaptable to the beginning or the end of a meal.

— FRANCINE
DU PLESSIX GRAY

Recipe for Sweetness and Good Fortune

As newly born infants, we clamor instinctively for the "gift" of milk and are rewarded with rapturous moments at our mothers' breasts or bottles lovingly held. We suck contentedly—growing rosy cheeks, plucky dimples and, eventually, a pair of swift legs whisking us from one laden table to the next. "Eat! Eat!" rings through our childhood, our appetites the source of both energy and great pleasure. We discover at a young age that food celebrates life.

This ceremony is dedicated to the bounty of the potluck. With your guests' offerings of their favorite foods, your table will brim with a profusion of delicious dishes. As we share and appreciate the good food, we invite the newborn to revel in the midst of our spirited feast and wishes for his sweet, auspicious life.

Gratitude Blessing

PARENTS *step up to the table, hold hands, face each other, and say:*

Thank you for joining me in the creation of our beloved new son, Lucas [your baby's name].

Thank you for bringing joy to our family and friends with this blessed occasion.

Thank you for the perfect peace I feel inside as we celebrate Lucas' arrival.

Thank you for the inspiration you give me to live with great purpose.

Thank you for everything I learn from you each and every day.

Thank you for being who you are and loving who I am.

Thank you, thank you, for this good fortune.

Thank you.

Blessing over Bread

PARENT *holds a loaf of bread and says:*

This bread represents the abundance of the table and is a symbol of gratitude and reciprocity. May Lucas always enjoy the pleasures of sharing a meal with loved ones.

HONORED CHILD carries the bread around the room and everyone breaks off a piece to eat.

GIFT OF FOOD

Collect non-perishable food from your guests and make a donation to a local food bank in honor of your baby's birth.

Drape a simple, white cloth over your dining room table. Place a flower arrangement that incorporates decorative seasonal fruits and vegetables in the center. Set out a pair of silver candlesticks holding orange candles (symbolic of comraderie). Wrap utensils in napkins and place them in ceramic jugs. Stack plates in one corner of the table. As your guests arrive, watch the table overflow with the color and serendipity of potluck.

Concoctions for a Sweet Life

★ A piece of baked apple placed in the baby's mouth sanctifies the baby's right to live. *(Germany)* ★ Strings of fruit and candy are attached along with small candles to a stick to honor good children. Candy-coated almonds represent the bitter and sweet of life. *(Greece)* ★ Sugar-coated anise seeds (pink and white for girls, blue and white for boys) sprinkled on biscuits spread with butter symbolize good luck. *(Holland)* ★ Cooked chickpeas, peeled coconut, and cookies are placed around the inner edge of the baby's cradle for protection. *(Bene Israel community of India)* ★ Apples ensure health, honey for sweetness, wine for happiness, and parsley for beginnings. *(Judaism)* ★ Almonds symbolize the essence of life. *(Mexico)* ★ Walnuts, almonds, raisins, and figs are ingredients for *kooree-shaat,* a special sweet given to children. *(Morocco)* ★ Meat cooked in sugar makes the baby sweet-tempered. *(Muslim)* ★ Dried fruit

or little plaques of peccary bone decorated with family symbols are attached to the baby's sling for protection. *(Matsi Genka of Peru)* ★ Pudding made from flour, butter, and sugar *(kara parshad)* is eaten at the baby's welcome ceremony two weeks after birth. Sugar water *(amrit)* is given to the baby as a symbol of purity, sweetness, and goodness. *(Sikh)* ★ "New-male cakes" are offered at temple during the *Making Happiness Festival* by mothers of newborn sons. *(Taiwan)* ★ Rice, symbolizing protection for the young baby, is mixed with raisins and butter and then eaten or thrown into the sky for an auspicious life. *(Tibet)* ★ Slices of a *slava* loaf are dipped in red wine and presented with an apple, a sugar lump, and basil sprigs to celebrate the baby's birthday. *(Yugoslavia)*

CELEBRATION
TOASTS

This circle within my home
is more beautiful
from the day
when it is given me to see
these faces I know and love.
All is more beautiful.
Life is beautiful.
I am grateful,
for these guests of mine
make my house grand.

—ADAPTED FROM AN ESKIMO
BLESSING FROM *THE WORLD OF*
THE AMERICAN INDIAN

Welcome to my feast.
I hold my family's hands
in mine and toast
the weaving of our lives.

In this house we
believe the finest blessing
is fine companionship
during a meal.
With such company
as we have now,
we are blessed.

— ROBERT FULGHUM

CHILDREN'S TOWER CAKE

This delicious work-of-art requires no baking. Provide a selection of colorful toppings and watch the children create a towering birthday masterpiece.

1 frozen pound cake, thawed
1 tin prepared cream cheese frosting
1 pint fresh strawberries (sliced)
  or fresh raspberries (whole)
16 oz. fresh or frozen blueberries (if frozen, thaw
  and drain)
(If berries are unavailable, substitute other fresh fruits such as melon balls, tangerine sections, sliced mango, or papaya. Avoid fruit that is very juicy or that turns brown.)
Chocolate sprinkles, grated chocolate, toasted coconut

Slice the pound cake into thirds horizontally to make three layers. Dental floss, held taut and pulled through the cake will make a clean, even cut. Place each layer on a sheet of wax paper. Frost the top and four edges of each. Invite the children to top the layers with fruit and sprinkles. Using a spatula, stack the layers of the cake.

Serves eight.

Welcome Toast

Gather your guests around the potluck table and pass out a glass of champagne or sparkling juice to each.

ELDER *lights a pair of candles and says:*

We welcome Lucas to his life, this bountiful feast. We encircle him with food and love, providing nourishment for both his body and soul. What Lucas receives from us today and everyday are the ingredients for a meaningful life. Lucas, we love you. We hold you. We wish you the best that life has to offer.

Blessing Before the Meal

Let us be silent and mindful of all we are blessed with and for which we give thanks: family and friends, hope and health, happy memories and the food on this table. [Moment of silence.]
So, in giving thanks, we are blessed.

— ADAPTED FROM A TRADITIONAL CHRISTIAN BLESSING

*Behold our family here assembled.
We thank you for this place in
which we dwell, for the love that
unites us, for the peace accorded us
this day, for the hope with which
we expect tomorrow;
for the health, the work, the food,
and the bright skies that make our
lives delightful; for our friends in all
parts of the earth. Give us courage
and gaiety and quiet mind.*

— ROBERT LOUIS STEVENSON
(1850-1894)

*We sip the wine of hope,
toasting our baby's life, and savor
the sweet taste of anticipation
for the days to come.*

WORLD
CUSTOMS

★ *Britain:* Cake with white icing is served at baby christenings. If the baby is a first born, a piece of the parent's wedding cake may be placed on top.

★ *China:* Red eggs are incorporated into the naming and welcome ceremony when the baby is one month old.

★ *Ghana:* A drop of water and a drop of alcohol are placed on the baby's tongue to symbolize the difference between truth and lies and the hope that the child will always choose the path of truth.

★ *India:* Sugar cookies (for girls) or yellow fudge (for boys) are placed in the newborn's mouth at naming ceremonies.

★ *Italy:* Chicken soup, accompanied by *zaleti* (cornmeal cookies) and *grappa* (an alcoholic beverage) infused with dried fruit are served to well-wishers.

★ *Japan:* A single grain of rice is placed in the baby's mouth with a chopstick to symbolize his

acceptance into the community on the 109th day after birth.

★ *Korea:* Plates of food are passed to family members and neighbors on the baby's 100th day of life. The plates are returned with pieces of long white cotton thread draped over them to symbolize long life for the infant.

★ *Muslim:* Honey or sugar is put on the baby's tongue at birth and he is then blessed with a prayer.

★ *Nigeria:* A spicy soup made from dried fish, yams, and red pepper is served to the new mother to help restore her strength after delivery.

★ *Persia:* Rice cookies, chickpea cookies, and a variety of other sweets are eaten in celebration for seven days after a baby's birth.

★ *Russia: Pelmeni* (meat-filled dumplings), *piroshki* (dough filled with meat or vegetables) and vodka are served to the father's friends before mother and baby arrive home from the hospital.

★ *Muong in Vietnam:* During the first ceremony, the new soul of the baby is invited to come and eat. A bracelet of cotton is attached to the baby to link him to his new soul.

Closing Prayer

And now, O friends,
hear the dream of a word:
Each spring gives us life,
the golden ear of corn refreshes us,
the tender ear of corn becomes a
necklace for us.
We know that the hearts of our
friends are true.

—TRANSLATED FROM THE NAHUATL
(MEXICAN) LANGUAGE BY ADRIAN
BUTASH FROM *BLESS THIS FOOD*

〜 S I M P L E 〜
G E S T U R E

*Collect heirloom family recipes
that have been passed down through
the generations. Store them in a
recipe box to give to your child
when he leaves home.*

*...gather hony of each flowre, as doth the labrous Bee. Shee lookes not who
did place the Plant, nor how the flowre did grow; Whether so stately up aloft, or neere
the ground below. But where she finds it, there she workes, and gets the wholsome food,
And bears it home, and layes it up, to doe her Country good.*

—DOROTHY LEIGH (C. 1616)
FROM "COUNSELL TO MY CHILDREN" FROM *THE MOTHER'S BLESSING*

New Beginnings

We gather the sea in cupped hands,
blue jewel bathes the blossoming land,
reflecting the sun's applause
for the first touch of a baby's skin.

We hold the sky with pillared arms,
starry canopy crowns the pebbled path,
witnessing the moon's salute
for the first kiss from a father's lips.

We call your proud name, newly given
beneath the shimmering sky,
above the swelling sea,
gathering, where hearts greet
in the home of a newborn child.

My father was once walking on the beach with his three-year-old grandson when the little boy stopped, picked up a tiny fragment of a seashell, and began to examine it. My father bent down and, looking at the tiny fragment, he asked the boy, "How could you see such a little shell?" "Because," said the boy, "I have little eyes."

—THOMAS W. MANN FROM
TO TASTE AND SEE

I have never watched a clear morning awaken without exclaiming, *That is the most beautiful sky I have ever seen!* The blank canvas of the pure, dark pre-dawn bursts into a sun-drenched surprise of color and texture in a new way, every day.

Purity and Promise My appreciation derives from the same essence that all parents source when their children are born. Marveling at the innocence that each baby comes cloaked in, we watch the promise of its life blossom like a sunrise and know, *This is the most beautiful baby I have ever seen.*

This ceremony invokes the renewing qualities of water to sanctify your baby's arrival. It is especially lovely when conducted by the sea, lake, or pond, but even a birdbath or bowl of water will suffice.

...As water

so purify our spirits...

—CHRISTINA ROSETTI (1830-1894)

Welcome to the Elements

Invite the children to create a large ceremonial circle with seashells around the parents holding the baby. (If this is an outdoor evening ceremony, have them fill a large tub with sand and insert two dozen candles to make a "campfire.") When finished, children stand next to the baby. PARENTS greet the guests as they enter the circle.

CHILDREN choose their favorite elements of nature and take turns chanting a welcome:

Welcome, Cloudy Sky!
Welcome, Big Sea!
Welcome, Golden Sun!
Welcome, Wet Sand!
Welcome, Little Sandpipers!

MORGAN (MOR-GIN) *means "by the sea." (WELSH)*

Welcome Invocation

MENTOR *holds the baby, lights one of a pair of candles, and says:*

The light of this candle shows that you have passed from darkness into light. May you sparkle in your new world, Morgan, as the sun reflects on even the tiniest dewdrop.

Light the other candle and say:

We welcome you, Morgan to our world—our loving home. The light of this candle symbolizes your new beginnings and illuminates the joy that fills your family on this miraculous day.

Pass around a large shell. Each guest silently or verbally makes a wish for the baby and visualizes the best that can be for her life.

Every beat of your heart connects you to the universal Spirit of Water, which links you to the waters of our entire planet. The water that you drink and the water that flows through your body is the same water that was, at one time in the evolution of the planet, frozen high on the snowcapped mountains. The waters within you were once cascading down mountain streams to the sea below. The water inside you has been high in a cloud mass above the earth, has fallen as soft gentle rain, and has seen the bottom of the deep sea. The water that runs through your body has ebbed through the bodies of your ancestors and will flow through the bodies of your descendants.

— DENISE LINN FROM *SACRED SPACE: CLEARING AND ENHANCING THE ENERGY OF YOUR HOME*

CREATING
AN ALTAR

This altar is dedicated to the purifying and renewing powers of the sea, inspired by the ceremonial tables that Iranian families set out in celebration of Nourooz, or New Year. Drape a blue-green cloth over a small table, wall shelf, or mantel. Arrange the following symbolic objects:

★ starfish or a bowl of goldfish (sea life)
★ water lilies in a vase (plant life) ★ sprouted grain (renewal) ★ a mirror (awakening)
★ colored eggs (fertility, birth)

...Every new birth is a new beginning. Especially when that new birth is intimately connected with us, it becomes a revival of ourselves and our old hopes center around it.

— JAWAHARLAL NEHRU

Purifying Ceremony

Sweet incense or a sage smudge stick may be used in this ritual to cleanse and purify both the ceremonial space and the inner spirit. Stand in the center of the circle and light the herbs in a shell. Hold the shell up high in the air and move it in each of the four directions, beginning with the east (where the sun rises). Pass the shell around the circle, allowing everyone to breathe in the herb's aroma and wave his or her hands through the purifying smoke.

The seeds of the day are best planted in the first hour.

—DUTCH PROVERB

HONORED FRIEND: Today is a new beginning. This moment is a new beginning. In every moment, we start over with a clean slate. We are free. We are alive. We go into this new day of great possibility with renewed energy.

Blessing of the Waters

GRANDPARENTS *hold the baby.*
PARENTS *dip a water lily in the ocean (or bowl of spring water) and touch it to each of the baby's body parts, saying:*

Bless Morgan's forehead with intelligence and wisdom. Bless her eyes so she will see great vistas. Bless her nose with delicious and fragrant aromas. Bless her mouth for the enjoyments of tasting, kissing, and communicating. Bless her heart with deep love and a strong, steady beat. Bless

her arms for embracing friendship and love enthusiastically. Bless Morgan's feet so they will never tire and carry her happily through her days.

PARENTS *carry baby to the altar. Light two candles, walk around the table three times, then say:*

We present our blessed daughter, Morgan.

WORLD
CUSTOMS

★ Afghanistanis feed sugar butter to babies for the first six days of life to symbolize cleansing.

★ Aborigines in Australia "smoke the baby" to purify and mark the start of ceremonial life. A fire is made from konkerberry wood. Water is sprinkled over it to dampen the flames, then green leaves are placed in the fire to create smoke. The baby's hair, head, chest, back, and legs are misted with water and she is then held in the perfumed smoke for twenty seconds. No words or prayers are spoken as the act itself is considered the prayer.

★ In Europe, Roman Catholics and Lutherans baptize their babies on *Children's Day*. This tradition has roots in the Old World. Water, whether it be a river, a deep pool in church or a font, is a vital part of the ceremony in which the child is reborn into society, then presented to the community.

★ Western Macedonians use sprigs of basil dipped in seawater in their baptism ceremonies.

★ Blossoms are placed on babies' heads in Nepal as a blessing from the water Goddess Durya during the *Dasain* Festival.

★ A purification ceremony called *Bang-so* is performed in Tibet on the morning of the baby's third day of life (for boys) or fourth day (for girls). Incense is burned to cleanse the home.

Oh Great Spirit of the East,
I face you to understand birth and
new beginnings. I look to you
bringing forth a new day
and am reminded that life is about birth
—of babies, puppies, new seasons,
new ways of doing things.
Teach me the mysteries of Beginnings.

— RECORDED BY JOSE HOBDAY
FROM *AN IROQUOIS ORAL TRADITION*
(NATIVE AMERICA)

GIRLS: Chelsea (CHEL-see) means "harbor." *(Old English)* ★ Dylana (dah-LAHN-ah) means "ocean-born." *(Welsh)* ★ Fontane (fawn-TAN) means "source of water." *(French)* ★ Keida (KAY-dah) means "flowing water." *(Old Norse)* ★ Kenda (KEN-dah) means "child of cool, clear waters." *(English)* ★ Marina (mar-REE-nah) means "sea-born." *(Latin)* ★ Nerine (neh-REEN) means "ocean sprite." *(Greek)* ★ Talula (tah-LOO-lah) means "water sprays to sky." *(Native American, Choctaw)* ★ Ula (OO-la) means "jewel of the sea." *(Celtic)*

BOYS: ★ Deniz (de-NIZ) means "flowing seas." *(Turkish)* ★ Hali (HAH-lee) means "sea." *(Greek)* ★ Irwin (UR-win) means "friend of the ocean." *(Old English)* ★ Kai (kye) means "water from the seas." *(Hawaiian)* ★ Marino (ma-REE-no) means "of the sea." *(Latin)* ★ Marvin (MAR-vin) means "beautiful sea." *(Celtic)* ★ Nen (nen) means "ancient waters." *(Egyptian)* ★ Roka (ROH-kah) means "foamy wave." *(Japanese)*

Farewell Blessing

Deep peace
of rolling waves to you.
Deep peace
of quiet sands to you.
Deep peace
of refreshing wind to you.
Deep peace
of shining stars to you.

—ADAPTED FROM
A TRADITIONAL GAELIC BLESSING

Lullaby

Float on the water,
In my arms, my arms,
On the little sea,
On the big sea,
The channel sea,
The rough sea,
The calm sea,
On this sea.

—CAROLINES, ULITHI ATOLL

Circles of Love

At this moon table,
we hold the chain of hands:
mothers cradle babies reaching
fathers cradle mothers singing
ancestors cradle families
taking their place in the tree of life.

At this moon table,
I am the melody of my mother's song.
I am the rhythm of my father's dance.
Be still, they say, and listen.
You are the heartbeat
of the love of hundreds.

Open your fists
into embraces
Open your arms' length
into loving circles.

—JAMES BROUGHTON

Gathering Gratitude

When I close my eyes at night, I see beautiful moments—time reflecting in the luminous faces of my children. As play and discovery shape their days, I hear the footsteps of those who walked this way first, joining the patter of little feet. I listen to their stories in my children's lullabies. I feel their arms, wrapped around me and, in their eyes, I see the nature of circles. My life is blessed in circles—my children stand in the center.

This ceremony consecrates the relationship between your new baby and the people she to whom she will be closest throughout her life. Together you will create a space where your child can receive love and guidance and learn to return all that she receives. The dreams we hold for our families cast a brighter light when we congregate with others in celebration circles.

The center is everywhere. —FRIEDRICH NIETZSCHE

Presentation of Baby

Invite your guests to hold hands and cast a circle around you and your child(ren). In this sacred space, all energy will be directed towards rejoicing in your new baby. Pass a long piece of yarn around the circle to symbolize community unity, or pass a hard-boiled egg to represent the continuity of life.

PARENTS introduce the baby to each person in the circle:

Mother [your family member's name], I present Olivia.

Olivia, meet your grandmother, Donna.

The circle contains and protects. People gather around in a circle; they circle their wagons in a field. Circles of people, circles of walls, circles of cities.

— TIKVA FRYMER-KENSKY

Circle Ceremony

ELDER: As members of Lisa and Adrian's [parents' names] family circle, let us teach what we know about parenthood and community. Do we have a story we can share that illustrates how families abide? What nurturing qualities do we value that will help these new parents raise their children?

Record each person's name and response, arranged in a circle, on a piece of poster board. (Leave room for Polaroid™ photos that will be added during the children's activity on page 77.)

★ In ancient Persia, new babies
were welcomed by seven
women, who performed a
sacred circle ceremony. Each
woman held the baby in turn.

The first woman would say,
"Take it." / "What is it?" the
next would ask. / "A child," she
would reply.

Then the baby was passed to
the next woman in the circle.
The last person to hold the child
was deemed "the nurse," who
ended the ceremony by placing
the baby in the cradle and chanting a blessing over her.

★ Quakers pass the baby
around a circle, as do Iranians
and the Mbuti of Zaire, to
hold, greet, bless, and welcome
her into the community.

74

CREATING
AN ALTAR

*This altar holds objects of sentimental significance
passed from one generation to the next. Ask each
guest in advance to contribute a meaningful object
and as they present it, to tell a story of why they
chose it. Drape a small table, wall shelf, or mantel
with a cloth or handmade quilt. Arrange the heirlooms
you've collected and watch memories come alive.
Some suggestions:*

★ hand-knit blanket ★ ceremonial baby outfit
★ talisman or sacramental object
★ silver baby spoon
★ baby handprint or foot print cast in clay
★ old newspaper articles ★ bronze baby shoe
★ music box ★ framed picture ★ jewelry
★ first haircut or tooth pouch

Kisses and Wishes for Baby

PARENT: The most important gifts our community gives us are a sense of belonging, a past and a future, values, diversity, and helping hands. With this wine, we join together and fill our family cup with your love and good wishes.

Pass a goblet and a bottle of wine around the circle. Each guest pours a drop of wine into the cup.

GRANDPARENT: Olivia, I hope you will listen carefully to your own heart so you may follow a life that is meaningful to you.

PARENT: Olivia, I hope you will be powerfully loving and lovingly powerful and learn early that love is your best guide.

AUNT/UNCLE: Olivia, I hope you will find your dreaming place and share every dream with us.

MENTOR: Olivia, I hope you will commit yourself to positive action in our community and offer your talents and service with enthusiasm.

After the recitation, the parents and siblings take a sip of wine and a drop is placed on the baby's tongue. Present the baby to everyone in the circle. Each guest kisses the baby, then verbally or silently makes a wish.

CIRCLE (in unison): Olivia, we welcome you and offer you an honored place in the center of our circle of love.

ELDER *lights a long-burning candle, places it in the middle of the altar, and says:*

This candle will burn all day to commemorate our promise to love, attend, and support this new family for all time.

W O R L D
C U S T O M S

★ The Dagara of West Africa believe that children belong to their community as well as the parents. Each child's soul knows before birth what gifts she will bring to the world. It is the duty of the village to help the child fulfill her life purpose.

★ The Cherokee believe that a baby chooses her new family while in the "other world," depending on the sacred duty she is required by Spirit to fulfill, the cycle of learning she needs to complete, and the special gift she will bring to the tribe.

★ Tibetan infants with a strong grip are believed to grasp wish-fulfilling gems in their palms, including the gifts of talent, wisdom, and experiences from previous lives that benefit their new families.

★ In India, newborns' heads are shaved and the weight of the hair is given in silver to the poor.

★ Uganda villagers visit the new mother and baby with a gift of money for the infant to ensure a prosperous future.

★ The Quiché of Guatemala bring food and gifts to babies during their first seven days of life. On the eighth day, families welcome community members into their homes to feast and to kiss the babies.

★ Japanese families bring their infants to temples where they are given presents from well-wishers, such as protective toy dogs. The babies then eat their ritual first meals.

★ The Kwakiutl of northwestern North America organize a *potlatch* (giving) to celebrate birth. This is a large gathering during which speeches are made and large-scale gift giving takes place, followed by a feast.

★ In New Guinea, the Baruya people's traditional baby gift is a salt bar which is kept on the family's hearth to be used at the baby-naming ceremony.

★ The Muslims perform *zakat* (giving to people in need) as a way to thank God for their babies.

Closing

GIVE-AWAY RITUAL

Many cultures give something in return for a gift received from nature. This is a version of a Sephardic ritual in which the tray of Elijah the Prophet, filled with flowers and candles, is passed around the circle. Guests add money or slips of paper with pledges to volunteer their time. The tray is auctioned and the highest bidder donates his bid, the money, and pledges to a charity of choice in honor of the baby's birth.

HONORED FRIEND: We commemorate Olivia's birth with our gifts to those in need. Along with our happiness, we acknowledge that the world is in need of repair. We promise to commit our resources to making a difference, one small step at a time. We are grateful for Olivia's life. We are grateful for all of life. And we will demonstrate our gratitude with services offered by this celebration circle.

CHILDREN'S CIRCLE JOURNAL

Take Polaroids™ of each member of the circle. Paste the photos onto the poster board next to the guests' names and wishes for the baby. Make a decorated frame around each photo.

Go where you are welcomed.
Give when you are asked.

—SCOUT CLOUD LEE, ED.D.
FROM *THE CIRCLE IS SACRED*

Tree of Life

Begin me, then watch
my shy uncurling;
watch me spear busy earth,
toss my cocoon,
lift slowly
with the white fog
over fallen leaves and moss.

Watch my shadow stand.
Watch my roaming feet.
See me.
Take my hand and taste
the sun of my skin.

Perhaps when

a tree bears fruit,

it pays more attention to

its deepest roots.

Perhaps enshrined

in these ancient myths

are lessons that you see only

when they appear

at your doorstep,

wrapped in a soft

baby blanket.

—SHU SHU COSTA,
FROM *LOTUS SEEDS AND
LUCKY STARS*

I admire the fortitude and grace of trees: starting life tenderly as a curious shoot, quickly reaching skyward, strong and still, enveloped in lush greens, then later kneeling down to nourish earth and begin all over again.

Ring of Eternity

I watch my children grow under my tree's canopy of branches, where my dreams still dance with the dreams of our mothers and fathers and I ask myself, *How do I show them what lies in their deepening roots?*

This ceremony commemorates the living part of ourselves— the seeds of family that we cultivate. The birth tree we plant for our babies becomes a flourishing keepsake, a symbol of the circle of life from birth through eternity.

*Parvis e glandibus quercus.
(Tall oaks from little acorns grow).*

—ANONYMOUS

Welcome Address

ELDER: Looking at your faces today, I see the hard work and the love of all those who lived before us. I see a heritage that has been passed down through time. I see and I feel the joy of our shared experience as we welcome each other and baby Elan [your baby's name] to this celebration day.

Community of Caring

In advance, ask your guests to bring with them a photo of a beloved ancestor or living person. This group of honored souls wil constitute the community your baby is joining.

Place a small indoor tree on a table in your entryway. Fashion hooks from paper clips and hang them on the branches. Supply a hole puncher. As guests arrive, ask them to punch a hole in the photos, and hang them on the tree.

PARENT *lights a candle and says:*

Today begins our celebration of Elan's birth month. Together we will create a circle of caring and reveal the legacy that awaits him.

[sample] I chose my grandmother Sally to join Elan's circle. Every summer when I was a child, she came to visit our family and brought one tiny gift for every day of her visit. I do not remember the actual gifts, but rather the anticipation of the daily unwrapping, conducted on Nana's warm lap.

Each GUEST *repeats:*

I chose [name] to join Elan's circle. [Share a story or memory.]

WHAT TREES STAND FOR

Bay: *Glory*

Beech: *Prosperity*

Birch: *Grace*

Black Poplar: *Courage*

Cedar: *Strength*

Cherry: *Good Education*

Elm: *Dignity*

French Willow: *Bravery
  and humanity*

Holly: *Foresight*

Live Oak: *Liberty*

Magnolia: *Love of nature*

Orange: *Generosity*

Pear: *Comfort*

Pine: *Endurance*

Plum: *Fidelity*

Sycamore: *Curiosity*

Walnut: *Intellect*

Water Willow: *Freedom*

White Mulberry: *Wisdom*

—FROM *THE LANGUAGE OF TREES*
BY GAIL HARVEY

CREATING AN ALTAR

*The objects on this altar will be hung
on your indoor tree or placed in a ring around
your outdoor birth tree, symbolic of the age
rings in a tree's trunk. Choose objects that
represent eternity and nature's cycle of life.*

★ Bird house ★ Pine cones, gourds,
and acorns ★ Miniature gardening tools
★ Sundial ★ Vegetable ornaments
★ Fruit tree seeds and flower bulbs
★ Beeswax candles ★ Fresh or dried leaves,
herbs, and pressed flowers

*Keep a green tree in your heart
and perhaps the singing bird will come.*

—CHINESE PROVERB

Tree Planting Ceremony

Ancient cultures believed that trees embodied life and contained within them the spirit of nature. Trees were and still are chosen to mark momentous life passages and are often thought of as guardians—sources of nourishment and healing for the home and family. Choose a birth tree to plant from the list in the sidebar. If you don't have a spacious garden, arrange to plant the tree in a local park or in someone else's backyard. (If this is not possible, substitute a potted plant or an indoor tree such as a bonsai.) Prepare for the planting by weeding, amending, and tilling the soil per the grower's instructions.

E L D E R: We plant this magnolia tree [insert your tree] in our garden today to consecrate our joy at the birth of Elan. May our tree grow brave and beautiful as Elan grows. We will tend this tree and remember that love and children too must be nurtured. As

Plant one tree every five years. — BUDDHA

this tree and Elan thrive, we will remember these happy moments spent together.

Guests take turns digging the hole with a shovel or their hands. Parents place the tree. Guests fill the hole and tamp the soil.

Oldest child waters the tree using a watering can, then passes the can around the circle. As each person waters, invite them to verbally or silently "sow" good wishes for the baby and tell how he or she plans to watch over this newly planted tree and child.

Make every event in your life the reason to plant a living memory, a shrub, another tree, a climbing rose over an archway.

— DOLORES ASHCROFT-NOWICKI

WORLD CUSTOMS

★ The ancient Aztecs planted a tree at the birth of a child in the hope that the child would gather strength from the overflowing vitality of the tree.

★ In Switzerland, it is customary to plant an apple tree at the birth of a boy, a nut tree for a girl.

★ An old Jewish tradition is to plant a cedar tree at the birth of a boy, a pine or apple tree for a girl.

★ In Sweden, an addition to the family is frequently marked by the planting of a tree of destiny at the child's home.

★ On the Malacca Peninsula, families believe that the life and destiny of their babies are tied mythically to that of the birth trees they plant in semisacred enclosures.

★ Apache women gave birth under trees and placed their babies' placentas in the branches. When the leaves returned in the spring, the life of the person born there was considered to be renewed. Later in life, the person would make pilgrimage back to this birth spot to receive strength and vitality.

Inspirational Readings

We vow to love, respect, and cherish our baby. We will plant the seeds of hope and watch them blossom as we grow together in the wisdom of this new life. We pray for sound judgment in all our parenting decisions and in moments of darkness, we aspire to live in the light of the moon and sun.

—ADAPTED FROM PSALM 61

Hold on to what is good,
even if it is a handful of earth.
Hold on to what you believe,
even if it is a tree which stands by itself.
Hold on to what you must do,
even if it is a long way from here.
Hold on to life,
even when it is easier letting go.
Hold on to my hand,
even when I have gone away from you.

—PUEBLO VERSE

GIRLS: Adoette (ah-do-AY-tuh) means
"strong as a tree." *(Native America)* ★ Alani
(ah-LAH-nee) means "orange-bearing tree."
(Hawaii) ★ Ashley (ash-lee) means "from the
field of ash trees." *(Old English)* ★ Bel (bell)
means "revered tree known as wood apple."
(Hindi) ★ Carmela (kar-MAY-lah) means
"bountiful orchard." *(Italy)* ★ Daphne
(DAFF-nee) means "laurel tree." *(Greece)*

BOYS: Barclay (BARK-lay) means "birth-
tree meadow." *(Scottish)* ★ Dekel (DEH-
kehl) means "swaying palms or date-bear-
ing trees." *(Swahili)* ★ Lennox (LEN-icks)
means "with many elm trees." *(Scottish Gaelic)*
★ Lindell (LIN-dell) means "from the linden
tree dell." *(Teutonic)* ★ Orji (OR-jee) means
"majestic trunk." *(Nigerian Ibo)* ★ Perry
(PAYR-ee) means "pear-bearing grove."
(France) ★ Seldon (SELL-dun) means "val-
ley of whispering willows." *(Old English)*

Children's Tree Meditation

*Gather the children around you in a quiet
spot in the garden or house. Invite the grown-
ups to make an outer circle. Read
aloud this guided meditation:*

Imagine you are the tallest
tree in the forest and how warm your
branches feel in the sun's bright rays.
Wave at the birds flying by and invite
them to make nests in your crannies.
Rustle your shiny leaves and make a
hiding place for the singing birds. Dig
your roots down deep so your trunk
can stand tall and strong. Make a wish
for the baby. Place it in an acorn and
give it to a squirrel. Watch the squirrel
bury the acorn. Your wishes are filling
the ground with happiness. Promise to
take care of the wildlife nestled in your
branches. Ask the baby to promise to
water you, sit beside you, and hug you
regularly as he grows up.

Light the Way

Family,
teach me
the way of doves
peaceful, loyal,
yearning wings
flying the freedom
skies above.

Family,
teach me
what old oaks know,
quiet, steady,
weathered roots
lining the brave
new road below.

May we walk
with grace,
and may the light
of the universe
shine upon our path.

—ANONYMOUS

Signposts

In my dream, I follow him down the stairs and out the door for the last time. This child of mine, who was born just yesterday, today steps out on his own. He kisses my cheek, looks up at the windows of our grateful home and then, silently, walks away, without me.

I awaken startled, as though from a bad dream, and jump out of bed. I find Jake, still asleep in his room, still a little boy. In my relief, I see the path of our good life together shining in a different light. The moments are richer, my presence more genuine, my hands more helpful, now that I have seen how quickly time fleets by.

This ceremony illuminates the signposts that we, as a baby's grown-ups, reveal to our children along the way. We are the guides and protectors—providers of roots and wings. This is our solemn pledge.

When wings are grown, birds and children fly away.

—CHINESE PROVERB

Welcome Address

PARENT: Welcome to our home, where the miracle of our baby, Jun [your baby's name] is filling us with a kind of happiness we did not know before. We have invited you to celebrate, not only this great occasion, but also the important roles you have played in our lives. We thank you for your presence along the way: for your strong hands and unconditional love, for your encouragement when we stumbled. Because of your guidance, we will be wiser and more loving parents, leading our son into his promising future.

Simple Truths Invocation

GRANDPARENT: In the name of Jun, we promise to search for what is true in every situation. In the name of Jun, we promise to tell the truth, speak kindly, and act wisely.

MOTHER: In the name of Jun, we promise to consciously choose positive thoughts and actions. In the name of Jun, we promise to encourage positive thinking and effort.

FATHER: In the name of Jun, we promise to treat ourselves and others with kindness. In the name of Jun, we promise to create supportive communities.

ELDER: We invoke these promises and hope that truth will teach us a better way.

If the beginning is good, the end must be perfect.

— BURMESE PROVERB

CREATING
AN ALTAR

This altar is inspired by the "art of placement" called Feng-Shui *(fung-shway), which focuses on the objects we surround ourselves with and the positive influence they exert on our lives. Draw a ba-gua, as shown below, on a white sheet of paper. Tape it onto your table.*

wealth abundance	fame self-expression	relationships marriage
family ancestors heritage	health energy	children projects
inner knowledge self-realization	career path	helpful people guardians

THIS BA-GUA (GRID) CORRESPONDS TO
THE SPIRITUAL ASPECTS OF LIFE.

Arrange symbolic objects in the appropriate squares. Here are some suggestions:

★ bowl of rice or grains (wealth and abundance) ★ pearls (fame, self-expression) ★ framed photo of loved ones (relationships, marriage) ★ old key (family, ancestors, heritage) ★ crystal goblet (health, energy) ★ blooming orchid (children, projects) ★ heart-shaped stone (inner knowledge, self-realization) ★ feather (career path) ★ angel statue (helpful people, guardians)

Ceremony of the Mentor

An important part of many naming and christening ceremonies is the announcement of the child's Mentor (also known as Godparent), a wise and trusted person who promises to offer the child love and guidance on a continual basis.

PARENT: I know that Jun will become what he sees. The greatest gift we can give him is the presence of a loving and supportive network of friends and family. Let us pledge together to be what we wish for him.

We have asked Jun's Mentor, Thomas [name of person] to accept the honor and responsibility of caring about and guiding him through his life. Thomas, we ask you to give Jun the best of yourself. May you be strong, peaceful, patient, forgiving, faithful, dependable, and wise.

Thomas, will you love Jun? *(I will.)*
Will you guide him? *(I will.)*
Will you respect him? *(I will.)*
Will you protect him? *(I will.)*
Will you discover him? *(I will.)*
Will you lead him? *(I will.)*
Will you follow him? *(I will.)*

Thank you, Thomas, for pledging your love and attention to Jun.

What the child sees, the child does.
What the child does, the child is.

—IRISH PROVERB

W O R L D
C U S T O M S

★ Algiers midwives pretend to take thorns from the babies' feet with a needle and repeat three times, "I take the thorns from your path."

★ As a baby is born, Navajos chant a song called "The Blessing Way" to ensure that the newborn will be healthy, harmonious, and prosperous.

★ Hindus make sure their babies are on the right path from the beginning. During sixteen ceremonies called *samskaras*, the steps along the path of life are sanctified. For example, after delivery, *Aum* is written on the infant's tongue with a pen dipped in honey. Ten days after birth, the baby is given its name. The first time the baby is taken outside to see the sun is also a special occasion.

★ Muslim fathers set their babies on the right path by welcoming them with the Call to Prayer or *Adhan*, whispered into the right ear, then the left ear.

★ Buddhist monks come to the houses of newborns to chant and bless the babies. Sacred threads are tied around the child's wrist at one month of age to welcome a spirit called *khwan* who looks after the baby.

★ Japanese girls are given papier-mâché objects called *inubariko* in early infancy, which remain near their beds through childhood, then accompany them to their husbands' homes as a symbol of fertility and easy childbirth.

★ Central American christening parties are given by the baby's godparents. All the guests are given *encintados* (colorful ribbons inscribed with the baby's and godparents' names).

★ Orthodox Christian priests mark the baby's forehead, nostrils, mouth, ears, and chest with holy oil in the shape of the cross, to prepare the child for life and bestow protection and strength.

★ After a group baptism in the Philippines, godparents race out the church door holding their god children; it is believed that the first baby out the door will display leadership qualities.

CHILDREN'S
BLESSING NECKLACE

Ask each guest to bring a bead to the ceremony. One parent holds the baby and accompanies an honored child around the circle with a sturdy piece of twine (knotted on one end). Each guest silently or verbally names a quality they wish for the baby, then adds their bead to the necklace. Later the necklace may be hung on a wall near the baby's crib in remembrance.

I have a dream that my four little children will one day live in a nation where they will not be judged by the color of their skin, but by the content of their character.

— MARTIN LUTHER KING, JR.

Closing Invocation

HONORED FRIEND:

Today we commit to deepen spiritually in order to guide baby Jun as he grows up. We pledge to create our lives anew, focusing positive thought and action on ourselves, our friends and family, and everyone around us.

We will protect Jun, a treasured and beloved child. We will share our wisdom with him so he will learn the gifts of the mind. We will nourish his spirit and provide him with comfort and peace. We will guide his hands to make good in the world.

Promise for a Welcoming World

And the child watched the sun
and listened to the wind,
looking out the window
at the treasures of the world.
And the child heard the welcome
ringing in the voices,
hopeful and courageous,
singing to the sea.
And the child's eyes saw clearly,
far beyond the village,
hands applauding children
playing in the sun.
And the child dreamed of friendship,
And the child's dreams were happy,
And the child dreamed of children
everywhere circling, circling for all time,
a welcoming world.

How Faith Communities Welcome Their Babies

*ASSEMBLIES OF GOD

Ceremony: Dedication Service **Purpose:** Parents publicly state intentions to raise child in the teachings of Jesus and commit to Christian living. Congregants are asked to be Christian role-models. **When:** Early infancy **Text:** New International Version of the King James translation of the *Bible* and *Hymns of Glorious Praise*

*BUDDHIST

Ceremony: Name-Giving **Purpose:** Parents give child's name **When:** Any age **Text:** *Sutras* (collected sayings of the Buddha)

*DISCIPLES OF CHRIST

(The Christian Church)

Ceremony: Blessing and Dedication Service **Purpose:** Community acknowledges the baby's presence and parents seal a covenant between themselves, the child's sponsors, and the community to guide the child. **When:** Early infancy **Text:** *The New Revised Standard Version of the Bible* and *The Chalice Hymnal*

*EPISCOPALIAN

Ceremony: Baptism **Purpose:** Baby is immersed in water in a font or water is poured on his head to signify washing away of sins. **When:** Any age, but usually early infancy **Text:** *The Book of Common Prayer* and a hymnal

*GREEK ORTHODOX

Ceremony: Baptism, First Communion, and Chrismation **Purpose:** Baby is anointed with oil on the forehead, cheek, hands, and feet, which signifies the forgiveness of her sins. Wine and bread (symbolic of the blood and body of Jesus Christ) are given to the baby to underscore the importance of her future participation in the sacramental life of the church. The ceremony marks her initiation into the church. **When:** Early infancy **Text:** *The Divine Liturgy of St. John Chrysostom*

★ HINDU

Ceremony: Naming Ceremony (Rice-Eating Ceremony) **Purpose:** Baby is given his name and his first intake of solid food is celebrated. **When:** Six to eight months old **Text:** No standard books are used.

★ ISLAM

Ceremony: *Akikah* (ah-KEE-kah) **Purpose:** Baby is welcomed. **When:** Newborn **Text:** None

★ JEWISH

Ceremony: *Brit* (breet) "covenant" **Purpose:** The *brit milah* (breet mee-LAH) is the circumcision ceremony for boys, which signifies the covenant between God and the Jewish people. The baby boy is given his Hebrew name. Jewish girls are given their Hebrew names during the *brit bat* (covenant of the daughter) or the *sim-chat bat* (joy of the daughter). **When:** Eighth day of life (brit milah) or no later than fortieth day of life. **Text:** The *sid-dur* (SEE-dor) "prayerbook"

★ LUTHERAN

Ceremony: Baptism **Purpose:** Baby is initiated into the Lutheran Church and the Christian faith, her sins are forgiven, and she is promised eternal life. **When:** Early infancy **Text:** *Lutheran Book of Worship* and *Lutheran Hymnal*

★ METHODIST

Ceremony: Baptism **Purpose:** Baby is immersed in water in a font or water is poured on his head to signify washing away of sins. God is asked to strengthen the baby and the community promises to guide the child in the Christian way of life. **When:** Infancy **Text:** A bible and *The United Methodist Hymnal*

★ MORMON

Ceremony: Blessing and Naming Ceremony **Purpose:** Baby is blessed by the father and given his name. **When:** Newborn **Text:** None

★ PRESBYTERIAN

Ceremony: Baptism **Purpose:** Parents and congregation pledge to love and nurture the baby. God is praised and thanked for the new life. The baby is addressed by her name and immersed in water or water is sprinkled over her head. She is welcomed. **When:** Early infancy or any age **Text:** A bible and the *Presbyterian Hymnal*

★ QUAKER

Ceremony: Meeting **Purpose:** Baby's birth is celebrated. **When:** Early infancy or any age **Text:** A bible and a hymnal

★ ROMAN CATHOLIC

Ceremony: Baptism **Purpose:** Baby is incorporated into Christ and made a member of His Mystical Body. He is given the virtues of faith, hope, and charity and a character on his soul. His sins are forgiven, water is poured on his forehead, and he is declared baptized. **When:** Six to eight weeks old **Text:** *New American Bible*, a hymnal, and a prayer book

★ SEVENTH-DAY ADVENTIST

Ceremony: Baptism **Purpose:** Baby is immersed in a baptismal pool as a sign of remission of sin and spiritual rebirth. **When:** Early infancy or any age **Text:** None

★ UNITED CHURCH OF CHRIST

Ceremony: Baptism or Dedication Ceremony **Purpose:** Baby's birth and initiation into the church are celebrated and he is given God's grace. Water is poured or sprinkled on his forehead or he is immersed in water. **When:** Early infancy or any age **Text:** *The Holy Bible* (New Revised Standard Version) and *The New Century Hymnal*

Selected Bibliography

Baby Names for the New Century: A Comprehensive Multicultural Guide to Finding the Perfect Name for Your Baby by Pamela Samuelson.
(NY: Harper Paperbacks, 1994).

Birth Customs by Lucy Rushton.
(NY: Thomson Learning, 1993).

Circle Round: Raising Children in Goddess Traditions by Starhawk, Diane Baker, and Anne Hill.
(NY: Bantam Books, 1998).

Daily Affirmations for Parents: How to Nurture your Children and Renew Yourself During the Ups and Downs of Parenthood by Tian Dayton.
(Deerfield Beach, FL: Health Communications, Inc., 1992).

For Every Season: The Complete Guide to African-American Celebrations: Traditional to Contemporary by Barbara Eklof.
(NY: Harper Collins).

From Beginning to End: The Rituals of Our Lives by Robert Fulghum.
(NY: Villard Books, 1995).

Great Occasions: Readings for the Celebration of Birth, Coming-of-Age, Marriage, and Death by Carl Seaburg, editor.
(Boston: Beacon Press, 1968).

The Healing Wisdom of Africa: Finding Life Purpose through Nature, Ritual, and Community by Malidoma Patrice Somé.
(NY: Jeremy P. Tarcher/Putnam, 1998).

How to Be a Perfect Stranger: A Guide to Etiquette in Other People's Religious Ceremonies by Arthur J. Magida, editor.
(Woodstock, Vermont: Jewish Lights Publishing, 1996).

BIBLIOGRAPHY *continued*

The Jewish Baby Book by Anita Diamant (Woodstock, Vermont: Jewish Lights Publications, 1994).

The Language of Flowers by Gail Harvey. (NY: Gramercy Books, 1995).

Prayers for a Thousand Years by Elizabeth Roberts and Elias Amidon, editors. (SF: HarperSanFrancisco, 1999).

The Tibetan Art of Parenting by Anne Hubbell Maiden and Edie Farwell. (Somerville, MA: Wisdom Publications, 1997).

Religions of the World: The Illustrated Guide to Origins, Beliefs, Traditions & Festivals by Elizabeth Breuilly, Joanne O'Brien, Martin Palmer and Consultant Editor, Professor Martin E. Marty. (NY: Facts On File, Inc., 1997).

Welcoming the Soul of a Child: Creating Rituals and Ceremonies to Honor the Birth of Our Sons and Daughters by Jill E. Hopkins. (NY: Kensington Books, 1999).

★ Thank You ★

To our circle of supporters and well-wishers, we offer our appreciation for your presence in our lives:

Our families, for loving us and doing extra to make this happen; our friends, for your enthusiasm and patience; Kristin Joyce and Barbara Moulton, our agents, for believing in our creative spirits; Hazel Kleingrove for finding the word "Welcome" in twenty-one languages; Lisa Moresco, Michele Mason and Natural Resources, for nurturing families with babies; Alison, Gravity, and James of Phoenix Books for generous access to a wide array of research books; Lara Starr, for inspired editing; Mary Sullivan, for your vision; and to our entire team at Cedco Publishing, we accomplished this magnificently, thanks to your effort and guidance.

 A wide selection of trees is available at your local nursery or through the National Arbor Day Foundation.

888-448-7337 ★ 100 Arbor Avenue ★ Nebraska City, NE 68410

Ambledance Studios is the creative workshop of Andrea Alban Gosline and Lisa Burnett Bossi. We create inspirational books, calendars, journals, cards, and treasures for mothers, their children, and the families who cherish them. Our mission is to reveal a *welcoming world* where the promise of every new life is celebrated. We believe that the words we say, the intentions we make, and the actions we take in our babies' first years, shape their lives —and our families —for all time.

ANDREA ALBAN GOSLINE is an award-winning poet/author and is the Creative Director of *Ambledance Studios*. Her inspirational writings are crafted in a voice that is both plain-spoken and heartfelt, weaving in nature themes and her gratitude for motherhood and family time.

A native San Franciscan, Andrea lives in a 1908 Victorian with her husband, Carl and their two beloved children, Jake and Lily.

LISA BURNETT BOSSI, is an illustrator and graphic designer and the Art Director of *Ambledance Studios*. Her enchanting paintings and award winning designs are inspired by dreams, nature, and wishes for a beautiful and compassionate world.

Her husband, Adrian, is renovating their first home in Brunswick, Maine, that they will share with their daughter Lila, and two black cats.

LEFT TO RIGHT: LILA, LISA, ANDREA AND LILY

AMBLEDANCE STUDIOS

415-978-0816 ★ FAX 415-641-4181

www.ambledance.com

e-mail ★ andrea@ambledance.com

lisa@ambledance.com

♥

To every precious child, we send this welcome kiss.